An Auchmithie Childhood

An Auchmithie Childhood

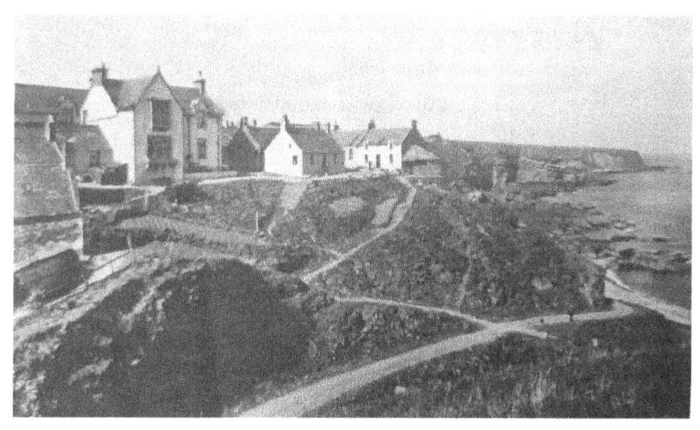

MARGARET HORN

ISBN: 978-1-78324-385-3

CONTENTS

Acknowledgements vii
Foreword viii
Introduction 1
Hearth and Home 3
Food for the Table 4
Water – The Very Essence of Life 5
Heating and Lighting 7
The BBC Home Service 9
Working Life 10
Managing the Household Economy 11
Transport 12
Entertainment 13
Weddings 14
At the End of Life 15
The War Years 1939-45 16
The War Effort – And Daily Life 19
The War Effort in Feeding the Nation – And in Putting Food on the Table 21
In Memory's Kitchen 22
War – Right on the Doorstep 24
VE Day and the Post-War Era 26

ACKNOWLEDGEMENTS

Compiled and written by Pat Clegg
with assistance from Seonaid McGurk

Front cover image and drawings by Rikki Craig

Photograph of Margaret in fisher
costume courtesy of Ann Craig

Family photographs – the Horn Family

Auchmithie Church 2025 photograph
courtesy of Seonaid McGurk

The team at Wordzworth
for their invaluable advice and assistance

FOREWORD

The germ of the idea to create this little volume was born out of the ever increasing requests Margaret was receiving from local organisations and societies inviting her to come and share her memories of growing up in Auchmithie in a period which is now part of a bygone age but which remains a treasured heritage.

The record of these series of talks now forms the basis of this illustrated narrative (the compilation of which is also the result of a team effort) the topics and stories chosen by Margaret to provide an insight into the very essence as well as the sheer physical grind of everyday life in a fishertoun community, grounded in a centuries old way of life and ancient traditions which also maintained close ties with the surrounding farming community.

It's the story of Auchmithie seen through the eyes of a small child blessed with an acutely observant eye and a sharp ear for the absurd and the incisive pawky humour which so often arose out of everyday situations.

The story vividly records the comfort to be derived from living on a diet of well cooked fresh simple fare, a childhood lived within a secure and warm welcoming home – and in accumulating an array of practical skills which she was to carry forward with such amazing and successful effect into adulthood.

Thank you, Margaret, for so generously sharing such a treasure trove with the world at large – of lives lived in all its elements and through a period of world shaking events – a past viewed through the trusting and accepting eyes of a well loved child.

Pat Clegg
2025

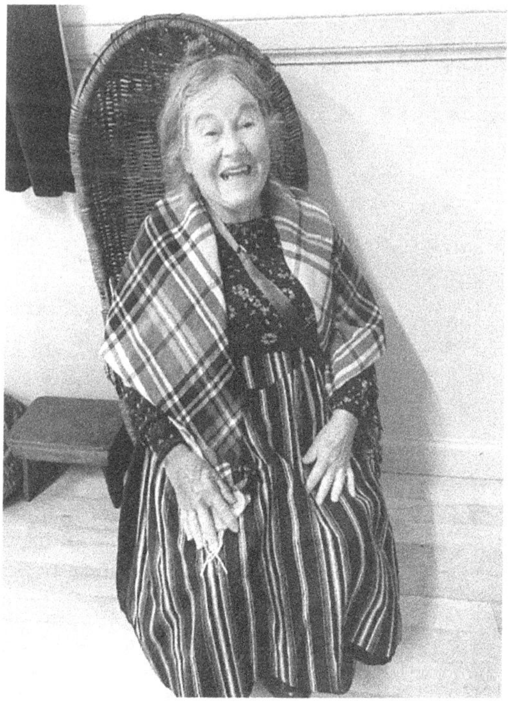

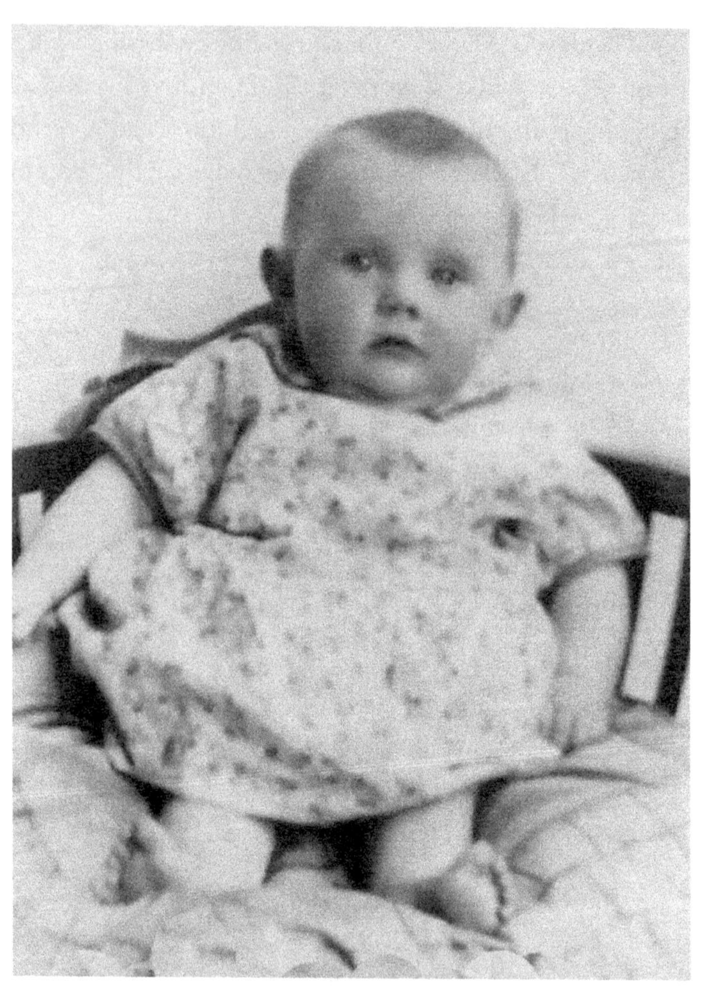

Baby Margaret, 1936.

INTRODUCTION

In its day to day life, the world that Margaret was born into on 7 December, 1935, differed little in many ways from that which would have been familiar to her mother, Meg Spink, born in 1896, a child of the late Victorian era. The pace of change then and in the early decades of the new 20th century would prove sedate in comparison to its later years.

Perhaps the most defining change locally in the early decades of the new century was the transfer of the ownership of the village from The Earldom of Northesk to the Grant family in 1919. The Grants, in their turn, were to hold the titles of a significant part of the village until well into the second half of the 20th Century until they, in turn, sold them to Angus Housing Association thus creating the village structure as it is known today.

Reflecting on her own Auchmithie childhood , Meg Chalmers would recall the childhood picnics from by-gone days, hosted by Lady Northesk at Ethie Castle, when all the children were obliged to turn up for the occasion armed with their own tin mug.

(Vestiges of the period of the Northesk earldom's ownership remain visible today in the Carnegie Armorials, still in pride of place on the frontage of what was previously the Northesk Arms, later renamed the Auchmithie Hotel. And, on a smaller scale but still visible, carved armorials sited between 36 and 37 Auchmithie and 44 and 45 Auchmithie and a plaque on the facade of The Steadings bearing the initials "WH" memorialising their construction by the 8th Earl, William Hopetoun Carnegie, 1794-1878.)

Hearth and Home

Heating and cooking was done on solid cast iron kitchen ranges with a tank to heat water on one side and with the oven on the opposite side of the central grate. Temperatures to either side were regulated by the use of dampers – levers set on each side of grate

A swey attached to the ingleneuk with hooks to suspend cooking pots would be moved back and forth across the fire to regulate temperatures.

Bannocks would be finished off after being firstly baked on a griddle by inserting the each individually onto a brander to toast off gently in front of the fire to ensure crispness.

The alchemy of cooking and the quality of the finished product was hugely dependent on the skills of the housewife in managing such a basic technology around the hearth – and, for the infant Margaret, would prove to be a lifelong influence and inspiration as she matured into adulthood and developed her own distinctive culinary skills.

Food for the Table

Tatties were supplied by nearby farms – as was milk and meal, the cornerstones of a rural diet and which constituted payment, in part, within the feeing process.

Gardens were situated all round the village, some right on the cliff edges, growing kale and leeks etc.

(In the early decades of the present century, the last vestige of "Hairy Spink's Garden" high on the clifftop and just below the field edge above the Monkey Den, provided the But n Ben with generous supplies of rhubarb each spring until the crowns were eventually subsumed by coarse grasses and smothered completely.)

Water –
The Very Essence of Life

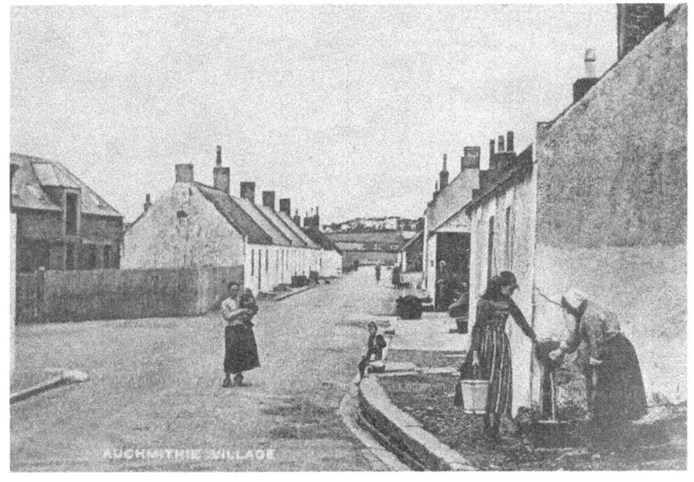

Note the white enamel pail used for drinking water and for cooking.

The water supply to the village was provided by outside taps situated at various key points with the water pumped up the Brae from the Beach. Water was then carried by the pailful to each property.

Wash-houses with their heated coppers were adjacent to the properties and the drying greens and the clothes lines sited around the village and, in the case of Number 24, situated on the clifftop directly opposite.

One doughty householder was to become the stuff of local legend as well as the butt of many jokes, insisting on washing bank notes of the day and hanging them out to dry on her clothesline.

Heating and Lighting

Indoor lighting was provided by paraffin lamps and candles. The more sophisticated and powerful Aladdin and Tilley lamps (which occasionally needed pumping to increase pressure and light levels during the course of an evening) still lay in the future.

Paraffin oil was delivered by Uncle Allan Smith, the village carter and scaffie, who was also responsible for the carting away and the disposal of human waste. And in collecting the spent ashes from the fires which were broadcast around the fields above the village.

AND IN A NEAT SEGUE TO ANOTHER TOPIC OF VITAL IMPORTANCE – "THE OAFFIES"

These were were L-shaped dry privies with double wooden seats with hinged openings on the rear wall to remove the buckets of night soil and waste.

Chamber pots, tucked away neatly under the beds, formed an essential part of bedroom furniture.

And toilet paper, consisting of carefully cut up squares of newspaper, was strung together and hung up on a nail in the "Oaffies".

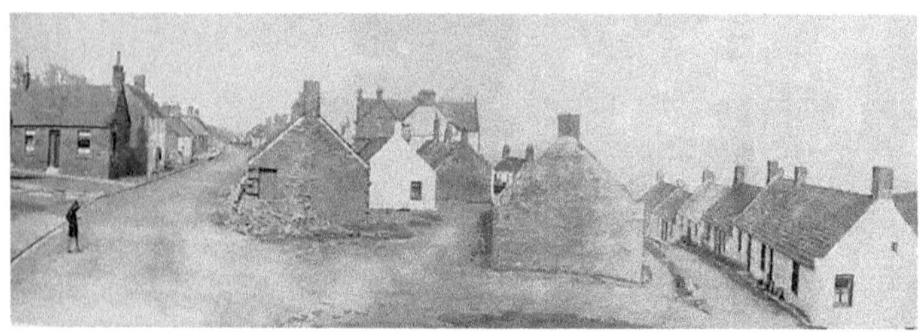

A view of the village pre 1950 with the ruined remains of no 46 and the internal connecting door still visible.

Margaret can recall No 46 being reduced to a "rickle of stanes" – forming a perfect playground for village bairns.

And a further point of interest in the continuous evolution of change – renovations to No 45 during the course of 2025 revealed long lost features – namely internal connecting doors between Numbers 44, 45 and 46. The form of the hearth of No 46 is now visible on the external restored gable wall – and evidence of a cottage lost to history.

This photograph provides a rare illustration of that period.

The BBC Home Service

Radios were powered by accumulators. The 9.00pm News marked the day's end and bedtime in a community where early rising was the norm.

Working Life

The majority of the menfolk were part-time – if not full time fishermen – apart from those working in a fulltime occupations on the farms.

There was a resident blacksmith, joiner, and roadmen as well as the aforementioned village scaffie, and a mix of fisherfolk and farm workers in the residential and social mix.

Men, women, and bairns were involved in tattie planting, clattin' neeps, tapin' and pu-in neeps, tattie howkin', hairsting as the seasons demanded – and in fishing and the production of smokies, processed to perfection in smokie barrels, and which were then conveyed by the womenfolk bearing creels around the towns and countryside.

Managing the Household Economy

Responsibility and management of the household finances lay with the womenfolk and money kept on the person – a "DOSSIE."

Transport

The primary mode of transport was "shank's pony."

The one solitary car was owned by Jock Robertson.

Bicycles had the benefit of lights powered either by a dynamo or a carbide battery.

Buses ran only on Saturdays.

Entertainment

Dancing was a favourite pastime with music in the Scots Tradition performed by musicians with squeeze boxes, moothies, playing the spoons for a rhythm accompaniment and, either lacking instruments, or simply in need of a change – in diddling competitions, a classic form of Scottish mouth music.

Tobacco, to judge by the wealth of surviving contemporary photographs of village scenes and in the abundance of fragments of fragile clay pipes unearthed around the village, was of great importance to men and women alike.

Weddings

Wedding ceremonies were conducted in the Manse and the Wedding Feast was celebrated in the Annie Gilruth Memorial Hall.

The traditional Wedding Feast consisted of Scotch Broth, Steak Pie, Trifle, and Cloutie Dumpling.

At the End of Life

Auchmithie was situated within the Parish of St Vigeans, another fact now consigned to history due to the recent radical restructuring of parishes and presbyteries within the Church of Scotland.

If a village resident passed away in hospital, the body would be returned home so that respects could be paid.

Then, on the day of the funeral, the cortege, accompanied by mourners would progress on foot along the Toll Road and the deceased then laid to rest in St Vigean's Churchyard.

The War Years 1939-45

Wartime in Auchmithie – reflected through the eyes of a child.

A community still with neither water on tap nor electricity and little in the way of motorised transport.

Margaret was four and a half years old when war was declared and almost ten by the war's end on Victory in Europe Day on 8th May 1945.

Margaret remembers with great clarity the night of 3rd September, 1939, when war was declared: her Dad's big chair situated at the left hand side of the coal-fired range with its swey; oil lamps and a paraffin stove providing further light and warmth in other parts of the cottage; and the radio powered by an accumulator.

Listening to the Nine o Clock News was an end of day ritual. But Margaret remembers how, on that momentous occasion, her mother burst into tears on hearing that Britain was once more at war with Germany. Small as she was, she was acutely aware that something very very sad had just happened.

Her father, Ralph, was an avid reader and kept abreast of news and current affairs via the Dundee Courier & Advertiser and the radio.

With a school year which began in August, Margaret

was almost four months short of her fifth birthday when she began attending Auchmithie School following the outbreak of the war.

Mrs Duthie was the then Headmistress, overseeing a school role of forty pupils, assisted by Miss Smart, a much loved infant teacher, in charge of the wee ones who were housed in the separate infant classroom.

The Head's husband, Mr Duthie, a veteran of WWI, suffered from what would now be classified as PTSD was called upon as necessary to administer the tawse.

Break times were signalled with a whistle referred to as "wheepie time."

The children returned home for their mid-day dinner break which usually consisted of soup or a piecie and cheese.

The girls wore uniforms consisting of kilts and jumpers which were changed immediately after school was out into "dungers" (dungarees.)

Following the end of the school day, the rest of the daylight hours were spent running free in a virtually car-less environment, playing hide and seek, skipping, ball games – and tapping in to a rich fund of bairn rhymes and games, a legacy which had been passed down through the generations – some of these bearing the hallmarks and oral traditions of a long and settled community.

As the war progressed, fifty child evacuees from Dundee were to swell the school role for a period as bombing raids across cities in the UK intensified.

There was a taxi service laid on to take older students to Arbroath High School.

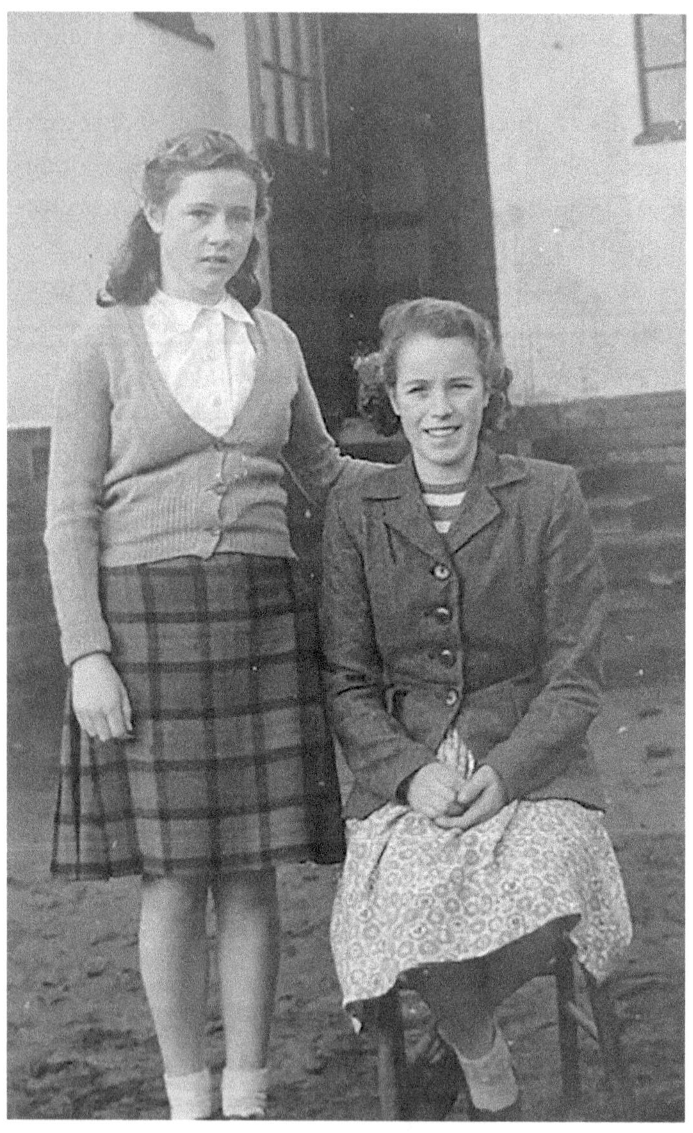

Margaret on the left in her school uniform.

The War Effort – And Daily Life

Margaret's mother, Meg, enrolled in the local unit of the Red Cross which was based at the school, and where training was delivered. Members of the Home Guard provided the "casualties" for the Red Cross recruits to practise their skills.

The Home Guard was formed by men in Reserved Occupations who provided critical skills and services in support and sustaining the nation's needs in the time of war railway workers; adults of both sexes working in munition factories; shipyard workers; fishermen and farmers and farm-workers tasked with keeping the nation fed at a time when the Atlantic Convoys tasked with bringing in vital food supplies were at constant risk of attack from the Luftwaffe and German submarines. And in serving in the Nation's defences.

The Home Guard on exercise and training sessions, suitably camouflaged and covered in greenery, practised their skills under the watchful eye of their Drill Sergeant – and under the even more watchful eyes of villagers who were able to enjoy a grandstand view from the Outlook – and who freely contributed advice and an often ribald running commentary.

"Look at 'Devvit' – a pin in ae hand – and a grenade in the ither!"

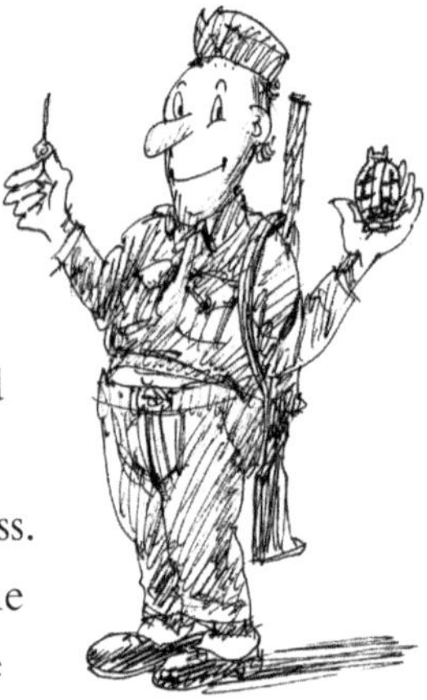

There was an Ack-Ack gun and a Searchlight sited at the Coasties.

A unit of the Free Polish Army was also billeted in the Hall for a time.

Wind-up field telephones formed a basic means of communication.

An ATS unit was based at Rumness.

The Auchmithie Hotel marked the check point where gas masks were inspected.

ID cards and gas masks were routinely checked on bus journeys.

Bomb Shelters, roofed with corrugated iron, were dug into the ground along Ethie Street.

Strangers, in general, were regarded with the utmost suspicion – like anyone briefly resident in the Hotel. Such inbuilt caution also inadvertantly netted the Minister from Carmyllie, whilst on a bird watching trip to Auchmithie and who was suspected of spying for the enemy.

Margaret's father, Ralph Chalmers, and the late Ron Reith's father, both farm grieves, both in Reserved Occupations, served in the Home Guard.

The War Effort in Feeding the Nation – And in Putting Food on the Table

The women folk, including Margaret's mother Meg, continued with their seasonal occupations working alongside the menfolk in the fields – all in addition to managing their homes and families: clattin' neeps; tappin' neeps; pu'in neeps; tattie plantin'; tattie howkin'; stookin'; and helping to bring in the hairst and the threshin' season.

Margaret's trips to Inchock, accompanying her father on the horse and cart, to collect the milled grain were to provide her with a store of truly golden memories.

In Memory's Kitchen

The family was provided with eight pints of milk on a daily basis – plus allowances of flour and oatmeal.

Daily fare might include, in season, sandwiches of thinned lettuce leaves regarded as a special treat.

Breakfast consisted of a bowl of milk placed on the table (the cream having been allowed to settle overnight providing a truly luxurious "mouth feel.") Porridge was served on a wide plate and the porridge laden spoon was dipped into the bowl of creamy milk.

Home made crowdie was a favourite and soor milk was used to make scones.

Margaret's Dad had a special fondness for Gorgonzola.

An all-time favourite – when available – was "Curly Kate", a sandwich formed from slices of a halfie (half loaf) spread with lavish amounts of butter and topped with slices of orange.

Hairy Tatties – a dried salt cod staple – was served up regularly by Granny Tib.

Meat based dishes featured as a teatime course.

Vegetable growing proved to be a vital and very necessary skill during the long years of the war.

Flagons filled with a mix of oatmeal steeped in water and stored somewhere to keep cool, made for a refreshing and energising drink whilst toiling away in the fields.

As an added and occasional bounty from the waves, barrels of lard and butter would wash ashore to be shared out.

Food Rationing, introduced during the War – and with all the attendant faff of clipping the tiny coupons from Ration Books – did not finish with the war's end. Rationing was to last beyond the Coronation of Queen Elizabeth II on 2 June, 1953.

War – Right on the Doorstep

"Germany calling, Germany calling". The nightly broadcasts by the universally detested "Lord Haw-Haw" were unsettling.

Convoys of ships being strafed and bombed out at sea were visible from the shore.

On a practical and local level, children were advised to dive into the nearest ditch and take cover if planes flew overhead.

Sea-faring, the bread and butter of a small fishing community, was strictly regulated for obvious reasons and catches constisted largely of partans, lobsters, and fish species close to shore.

A bomber, with eight crew on board crashed into the Ebbing Stane with catastrophic results, the bombs on board detonating with the force of the impact..

By way of contrast, a Spitfire managed to land safely – much to the relief of those watching the drama unfold.

In 1942, seven year old Margaret – along with the rest of Auchmithie's inhabitants witnessed "THE MINE" exploding, an event which became the very stuff of trauma remembered – and of legend – in later years.

In Fountain Square, Jocky Denty's swearing was epic and became a local legend in its own right.

The force of the blast blew fires out, extinguished paraffin lamps, and blew out windows along the length of the village.

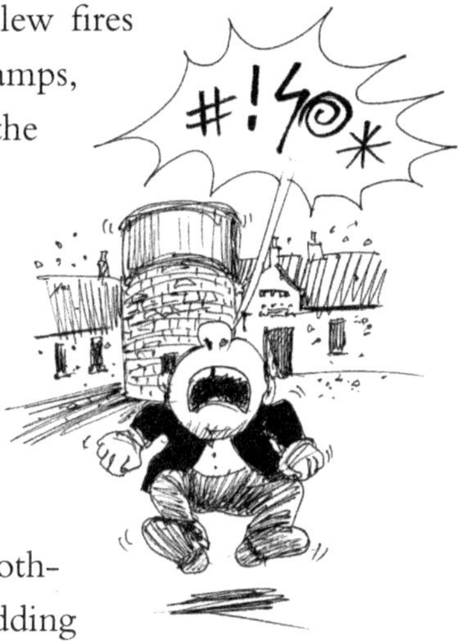

Margaret and her mother happened to be out when the blast occurred and her dad raced out hot foot to rescue them. Margaret remembers the sheer relief of being safe in her father's arms and her mother's hearfelt relief, whilst shedding tears of thankfulness, as they crunched their way home over shards of broken glass.

Sometimes it is the little things in life which trigger the strongest emotional reactions. In that particular devastating and fearful situation for Meg, it was the sight of her much loved epergne, shattered, and lying across the room in smithereens.

Margaret was a little four and a half year old tot when War was declared on Germany on 3rd September, 1939, and nine and a half years old when it was announced that hostilities would cease at 23.01 on Tuesday 8th May, 1945.

The war, at long weary last, had ended.

VE Day and the Post-War Era

On the day of the war's end, there was an explosion of relief – then sheer joy – as the news of the Ceasefire got out.

Back in Auchmithie, Fred Bennett set the celebrations in train by marching up and down the length of the village, using an old biscuit tin as a makeshift drum – which drew in crowds of youngsters, happy to join in the impromptu victory parade.

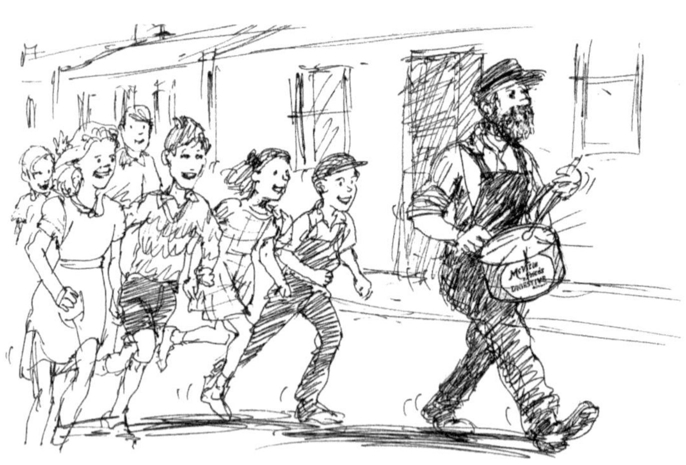

The village square was a time-honoured gathering place where people foregathered when news was to be shared – or in a celebration. Or in the joy of dance.

There is a distinct and unusual raised dais on the front of Number 19.This was the band's platform for dancing which took place on the square in front of the Hotel.

VE DAY celebrations ended with a massive bonfire down on the Beach when old and broken boats were torched and the grim days of The Blackout consigned at last to history.

Menfolk who had been on active service returned in "drib and drabs" following demobilisation which lasted for quite some time after the war's end. Coming from a centuries old fishing community, it was natural that a significant number from the area would have seen service in the Royal Navy.

Much of the post war period was tinged an aura of sorrow and loss. Lives cruelly lost on the very eve of the cessation of hostilities. Bereaved relatives wearing distinctive black diamond patches or black armbands signifying loss, many of them young widows and sweethearts.

Margaret remembers with painful clarity the sight of an absolutely distraught young woman running down the street clutching a telegram containing fateful news – news that no-one ever wants to hear.

And, close to home, Beenie's teenage son, who was killed after picking up a piece of unexploded ordnance which had washed up on the tide – that, sadly, despite many repeated warnings not to handle anything found on the shoreline.

Jimmy Forbes arrived home with a German wife.

The Swankies added a Welsh branch to their family tree.

School days, both in Auchmithie and later in the big school at Inverkeilor were, by and large, happy days.

Passing – or failing – "The Qualy" – the Qualifying Exam -at the end of primary school was a determining factor in the next stage of the education journey.

In the school playgrounds, boys and girls took part in their own separate games.

There was a similar divide in the classroom: boys had gardening; the girls sewing and cooking. Teacher, Mrs Carrick combined two rather diverse disciplines, maths and sewing.

There was also throughout all of that period, the usual range of childhood illnesses and infections to cope with – measles, mumps, whooping cough, diptheria – and the much dreaded TB as was the case for Billy Campbell at No 50 whose dad "was away in the war" and who had moved into Arbroath then sadly caught the fatal disease living in a house with shared toilet facilities.

The postwar period was to prove to be a time of accelerating technological and social change with the introduction of new mechanised processes in farming.

Horses and carts and horse-drawn farming equipment and tools were gradually being replaced with tractors and bogies.

However, it was still a period with no electricity or household water supplies but there was a public telephone in the village square.

The long bitter arctic winter of 1947 lasted long in the memories who managed to survive and live through it.

There was also a reluctance in a significant number of returning men to re-settle on familiar home turf, and opting instead for homes and employment and futures in Arbroath.

The "then and now" along the breadth and depths of a large rural community, largely dependent of physical labour, is perhaps most aptly illustrated by the daily School Bus Route and the number of pick-up points between Auchmithie and Inverkeilor : **Auchmithie >Mains of Auchmithie> Windy Hills>West Mains of Auchmithie> Seafield> Kinaldie> Boghead> Rosehill> Inchock>Raesmill> Ethie Mains> and so on to Inverkeilor School** by which time it was standing room only, the bus being packed to full capacity.

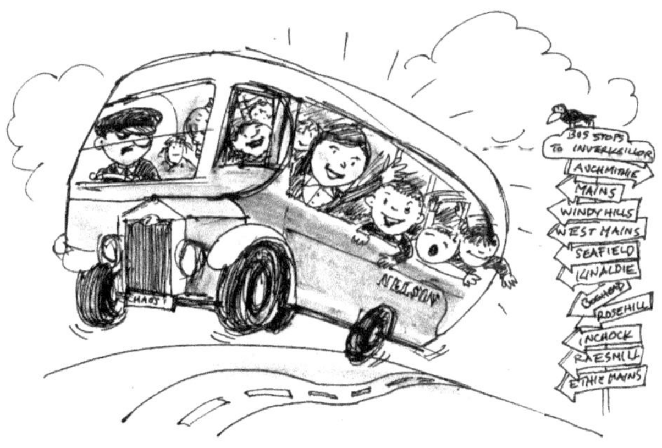

Car ownership was still something of a rarity and "getting a lift" was also something of a rare treat. Taxis were usually 'way too expensive to even warrant consideration.

However, there was one particular car-related incident which became the stuff of local folklore : a new red car (and proud owner) arrived in the village and, as an added treat, the children were allowed to sit and play in the car. Unfortunately, someone took off the handbrake and the car stotted all the way down the steps leading down to the Cart Road and the beach. Luckily, for the young occupants, a broken arm was the only recorded injury.

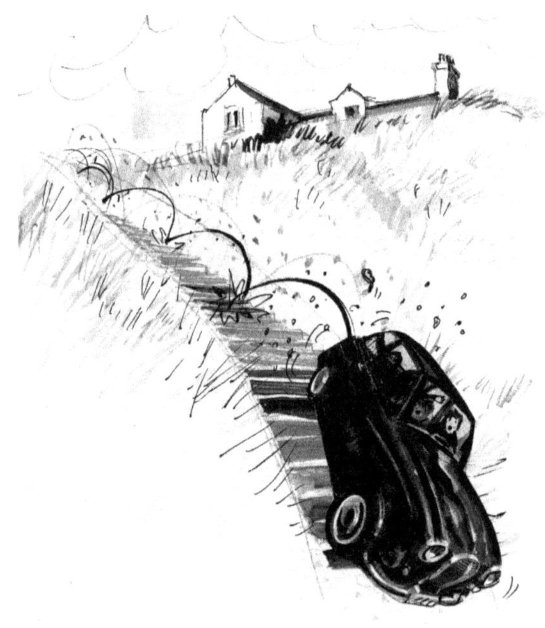

A new decade was to mark a step on the way towards adulthood and career options for Margaret's cohort with an almost inevitable move away from the village for some young adults.

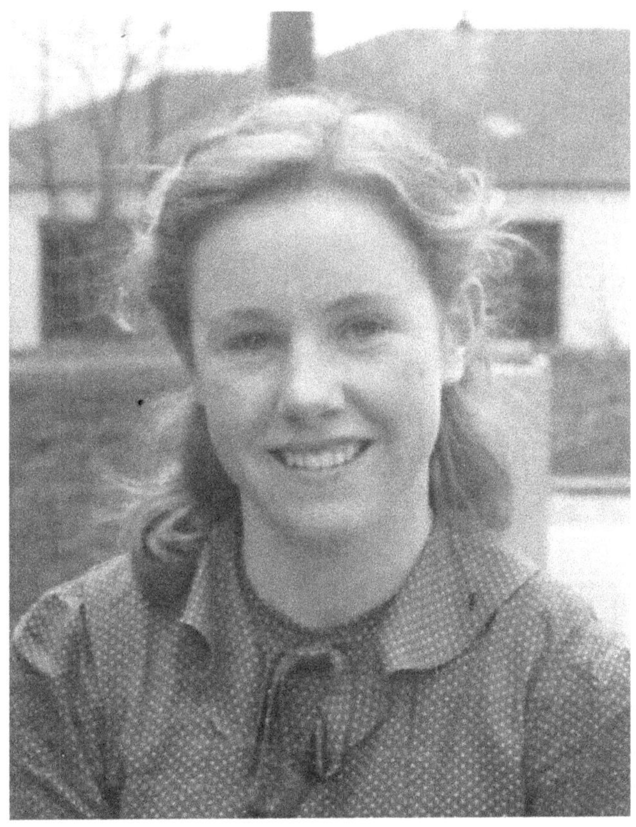

The teenage Margaret in front of the Annie Gilruth Memorial Hall

The Coronation of Queen Elizabeth on June 2nd, 1953, helped to brighten the social atmosphere with the beauty and majesty and dignity of the service – relayed to audiences worldwide via the magic of television and film – and the street parties held the length and breadth of the country – and across the then colonies and dominions to celebrate the occasion.

On 24th June, 1953, The Queen, accompanied by The Duke of Edinburgh, attended a service in St Giles' Cathedral where the Honours of Scotland were presented to the young Monarch.

But just in case the event might be misinterpreted as a Coronation, the Prime Minister, Sir Winston Churchill, had advised The Queen to dress down for the occasion – much to the disappointment of the crowds lining Edinburgh's streets including Margaret who, by this point in her life had embarked on her pre-nursing studies – and who had the benefit of standing on a perfect vantage point on The Mound. Margaret still feels cheated to this very day!

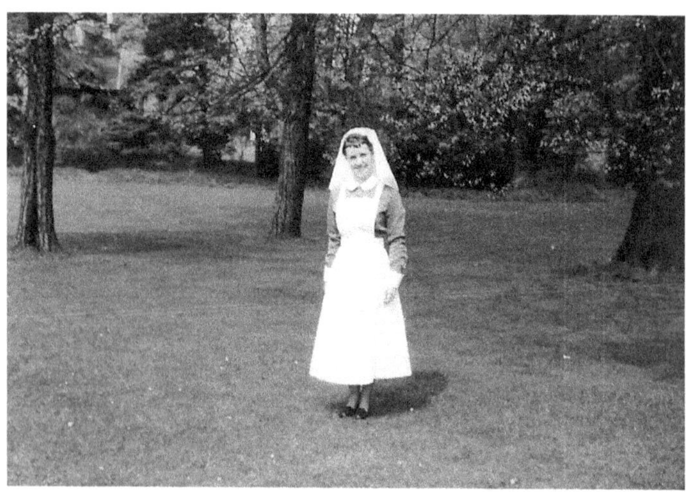

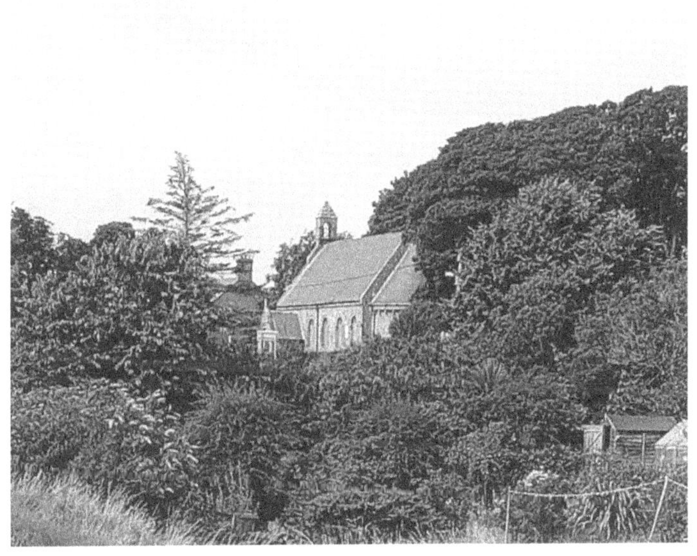

Auchmithie Church and in the foreground, Margaret's beloved garden

www.ingramcontent.com/pod-product-compliance
Lightning Source LLC
LaVergne TN
LVHW020313110826
845148LV00017BA/2646

* 9 7 8 1 7 8 3 2 4 3 8 5 3 *